EAST ANGLIAN STEA

VOLUME ONE

LIVERPOOL STREET

INTRODUCTION

The original London terminus of the Eastern Counties Railway—later the Great Eastern—was on the site now occupied by Bishopsgate Goods station. The present terminus was opened on February 2nd 1875, and consisted of ten platforms, now referred to as the West Side. Two of the platforms once connected with the Metropolitan Railway by the latter's Bishopsgate station; the only remaining sign of this link, which was subsequently removed, is a tunnel face adjoining the present L.T.E. Metropolitan station at Liverpool Street. Traffic expanded on such a scale that the existing ten platforms soon became totally inadequate and a further six acres on the East Side were taken to provide eight more platforms, bringing the total to eighteen. This addition was opened on April 2nd, 1894.

The station is operationally divided into East and West Sides. Platforms 1 to 10 on the West Side are used by the steam services, both main line and the suburban, to Enfield Town, Chingford and Hertford East. Platforms 9 and 10, the main departure and arrival roads, were until quite recently extended back beyond the end of the other platforms, under the Great Eastern Hotel, and these were the two longest platforms. Platforms 1 to 9 lead out to a separate roadway exit and in the circulating area beyond the platforms there are station refreshment rooms, booking offices and shops. The East and West Sides are separated by a roadway, and beyond the area of the platforms barrier of Platforms 11 to 18 is a further wide circulating area with stairways to the tube and to the street. This East Side of the station is wired for electric working and is used by the existing electric services, although some steam trains still use the platforms; it is the cleaner of the two sections of the station, although Liverpool Street is now within the City of London smokeless zone and special coal is provided for the suburban locomotives with a view to reducing smoke as far as possible.

A feature of the main line workings at Liverpool Street is the number of up locomotive-hauled trains which are turned round in the station to form departures. This reduces the number of empty train movements to and from Stratford and Thornton Field carriage sidings and also obtains a more efficient use of coaching stock. On summer Saturdays and during the period of the summer timetable, when a large number of additional trains are run, turning trains in the station is possible to a greater extent because of the frequency of arrivals and departures, although it is not always possible to equate public demand with operating improvements of this kind.

The Norwich via Colchester service provides a good illustration of coaching stock utilisation.

The other frequent main line service is that to Clacton-on-Sea and Walton, used by both residential traffic and holidaymakers. The displacement of the "Britannia" Pacifics from the Norwich service has made possible the allocation of some of these engines to the Clacton residential trains and notable improvements were introduced this summer, including a new named train, "The Essex Coast Express", arriving in at Liverpool Street at 9.20 and returning to Clacton at 5.27pm. The 4.58 and 5.40pm (previously 5.36) down have also enjoyed substantial cuts in their schedules, and the up residentials due in at 8.39 and 8.43 have been speeded up. During the winter the full interval service does not run, but in the summer there is an hourly service from 8.36am to 9.36pm. Most of the trains have buffet cars and some sets work three trips to Clacton and back each day in the summer.

Another long-distance service on the Colchester line is that to Yarmouth and Lowestoft, 122 and 118 miles respectively from Liverpool Street. This is much less frequent than that to Norwich or Clacton and the first train from the East Suffolk line arrives in at 10.31am.

Throughout the year there are two daily boat trains to Parkeston Quay for the Hook of Holland. A day service leaves London at 8.20am during the winter and at 9.05 during the period of summer time. This is the "Day Continental" and the return service gets back to Liverpool Street at 8.30pm in winter and about an hour later in summer. The train is a short set of about seven or eight coaches and is worked by a "B1" 4–6–0 from either Stratford or Parkeston depot. Another regular daily train, the "Scandinavian", runs in connection with sailings to Esbjerg by the Royal Danish Mail Route, departs usually at either 10.05am or 3.05pm, according to sailing arrangements, and arrives back in Liverpool Street at 3.00pm; again a short train suffices, hauled usually by a "B1".

The "Hook Continental", for the nightly boat from and to the Hook of Holland, arrives in London at 9.14am and sets out at 7.30pm in the winter or 8.00pm in summer. It includes a distinctive set with an interior laid out similarly to the L.N.E.R. "Coronation" trains. A "Britannia" Pacific is allocated to this train, as it loads to 12 coaches, and a Stratford engine goes down each night with a Parkeston crew to return with the up train next morning. At holiday times a relief boat may be run. Other trains from Parkeston Quay to Liverpool Street are the B.A.O.R. leave specials and parcels trains.

The Cambridge line carries several fast and semi-fast services to Hunstanton and March. The fastest weekday train is the "Fenman", which serves Hunstanton and Wisbech, arriving in Liverpool Street at 9.57am.

On the West Side one meets the remaining Liverpool Street workings which still arouse adverse comment. It is not the frequency of the Enfield and Chingford services that comes under fire, but the fact that it is still steam-operated and the rolling stock is not very modern. The end of what was once the most intensive steam suburban service in the world is now in sight, however, as the suburban services from Liverpool Street to Enfield, Chingford, Hertford East and Bishops Stortford will be electrified by 1960.

The trains to Enfield Town and Chingford are worked by "N7" 0–6–2 tanks, and the coaches are the Gresley 10-car articulated sets built for the G.E.R. area suburban services; the Chingfords have 10 cars in the peak and the Enfields five cars (on a few trains a single coach is added to make six). All use the suburban line to Bethnal Green, where some of the Chingford trains cross to the main lines as far as Hackney Downs. The Hertford East and Bishops Stortford trains offer both first and second class, and modern steam compartment stock displaced from the Southend line is now used, together with some B.R. standard coaches.

Two important newspaper trains are despatched from the station in the small hours. The first is a fast nine-coach limited-load train for Norwich, leaving at 2.55am and calling at Manningtree, Ipswich, Stowmarket and Diss. A 2,000hp diesel now works this train and returns from Norwich with the 7.45am "Broadsman". The second train, worked by a Stratford Pacific, leaves at 3.20am and calls at Chelmsford, Witham, Colchester, Wivenhoe and most stations to Clacton and Walton. Other newspapers are despatched by the ordinary early morning passenger trains and about 4,000 packages are handled each morning, 2,000 on Saturdays and over 5,000 on Sundays.

A wide range of motive power is to be seen at Liverpool Street, ranging from G.E.R. to B.R. standard engines. L.N.E.R. designs are very much represented, both by post-war types, such as "B1s" and "L1s", and the pre-war express engines of Class "B17". The largest express steam passenger engines are, of course, the B.R. "Britannia" Pacifics. Mention should also be made of the two station pilots – "J69" No. 68619, the East Side pilot, and "N7" No. 69614, the West Side pilot. Both are kept in a spotless external condition and are manned by three sets of men throughout each 24-hour period; the engines go to Stratford for examination on Sundays.

The stationmaster has a staff of about 500 concerned with the operation of the station and station offices. During a normal day about 154,000 passengers use the terminus.

At present, Liverpool Street represents three phases of railway operating developments; steam suburban services, modern electric suburban and outer-suburban services; and a main line service, mostly on a regular interval departure pattern, with a maximum use of rolling stock. All these three methods of operation provide unlimited interest, and time spent watching the operations at Liverpool Street is always rewarding.

An extract from "RESORTS FOR RAIL FANS" No. 25 by B. Perren, AM InstT, "TRAINS ILLUSTRATED" October 1958, reproduced by kind permission of Ian Allan Ltd.

ACKNOWLEDGEMENTS

In compiling Liverpool Street I have received enthusiastic assistance from F. Hornby, P. J. Kelly, N. L. Browne, A. J. Pike, R. K. McKenny, J. A. C. Kirke, A. E. Bennett, P. Hay, A. J. Willmott, B. I. Nathan, W. Cole and the dedicated staff of The Lavenham Press Ltd. In particular I would like to thank Frank Hornby, Philip Kelly and Jack Kirke for responding so readily to my requests, and for the loan of valuable negatives.

FRONT COVER

A sunny spring day – April 21st 1956, and Class "B2" No 61632 "BELVOIR CASTLE" arrives at Liverpool Street passing Class "B1" No 61003 "GAZELLE".

(*Photo* – N. L. Browne)

INSIDE FRONT COVER

A picture which encapsulates everything about Liverpool Street. It was taken in 1953, but could easily belong to any period during the previous 45 years.

(*Photo* – J. A. C. Kirke)

Published by South Anglia Productions, 26 Rainham Way, Frinton-on-Sea, Essex CO13 9NS

ISBN 1 871277 10 8

Printed in England by The Lavenham Press Ltd.

BACK COVER

Towards the end of G.E. steam "N7" tanks could still be seen at Liverpool Street. Five months before withdrawal No 69621 is pictured under the vast roof. The loco became the only member of its class to be preserved.

(*Photo* – J. A. C. Kirke)

INSIDE BACK COVER

G.E.R. 4–2–2 No 11, taken at Liverpool Street very soon after its appearance in 1898/9. It was one of 10 (10/19) built at Stratford for hauling the accelerated trains to Cromer and Hook of Holland expresses. These were the last single driver engines built for the Great Eastern Railway, and although they were running for many years the "Claud Hamiltons" (first of which No 1900) appeared in that year speedily succeeded the single wheelers.

(*Photo – courtesy* E. W. Griggs, P. J. Kelley collection)

THIS PAGE

L.N.E.R. splendour at Liverpool Street. A beautifully turned out Class "B12/3" No 8542 pilots a "Claud Hamilton" (later class "D15") 4–4–0 on an East Anglian departure during 1939.

(*Photo* – T. Spurge, P. J. Kelley Collection)

Above: An April 1948 view from a familiar vantage point shows class "B17" and B1" locomotives in typical smoky Liverpool Street surroundings.
(*Photo* – J. A. C. Kirke)

Below: A typical Liverpool Street scene during the late 1950s. Class "B1" No 61314 runs out for servicing, past an unidentified "N7" tank. In the distance a condensing Class "N2" waits at the high level approaches to Broad Street. May 10th 1958.
(*Photo* – N. L. Browne)

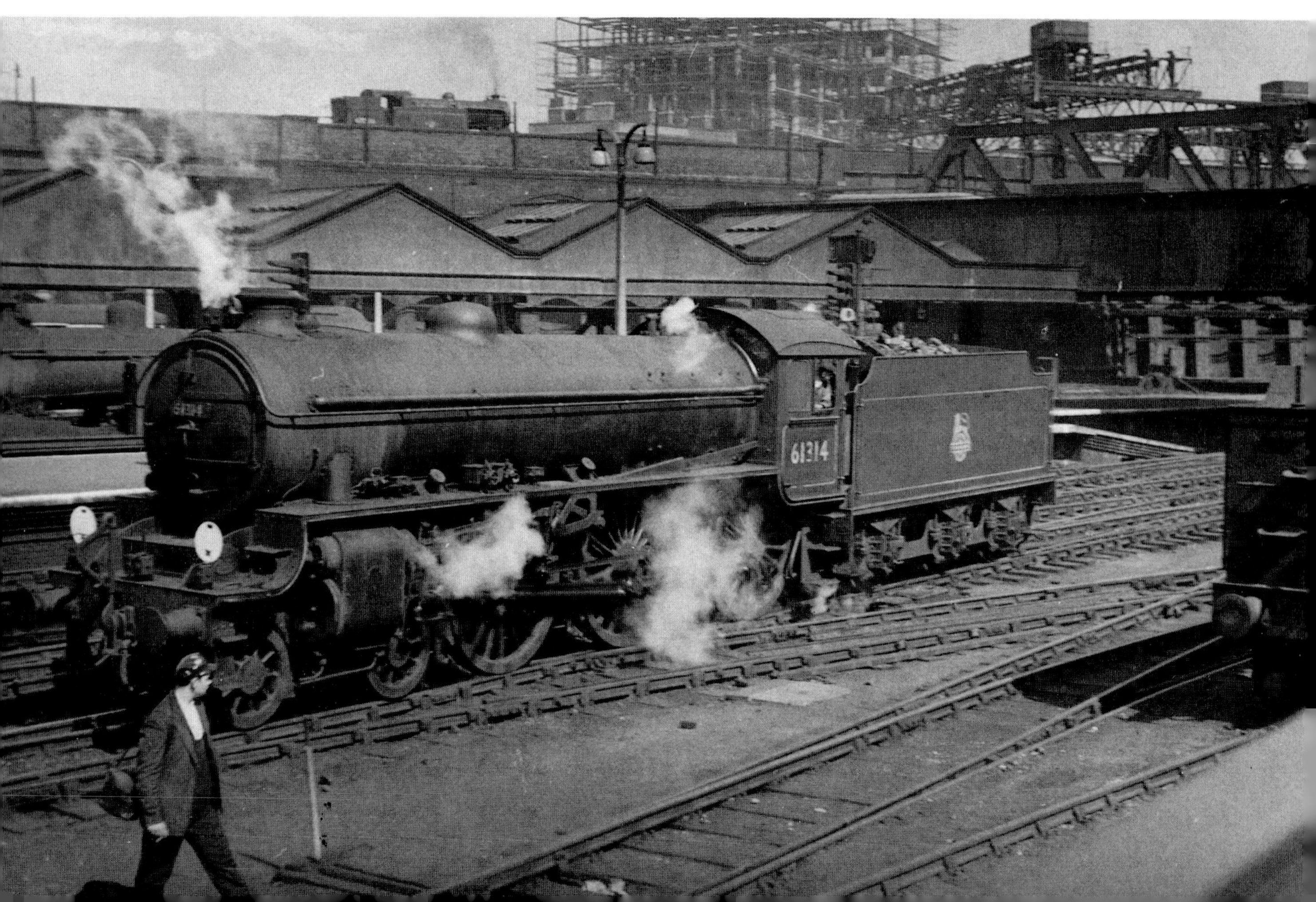

Above: Liverpool Street was famous for its immaculate Station "Pilots". West side pilot class "N7/4" No 69614 is captured between duties during April 1960. She was withdrawn later in the year. (*Photo* – A. J. Pike)

Below: With gleaming metalwork and bright red coupling rods, East side pilot class "J69/1" No 68619 was also photographed in April 1960, between assignments. (*Photo* – A. J. Pike)

Above: "Britannia Pacifics" were still very much a novelty when this photograph was taken in 1952." No 70007 "COEUR-DE-LION" waits to leave with the down "East Anglian". (*Photo* – B. I. Nathan)

Below: A Loughton–Brighton excursion is eased into Liverpool Street behind Class "J15" No 65476 on July 4th 1954. The train would traverse the East London line after reversal hauled by two class "J69" tanks. (*Photo* – P. J. Kelley)

Above: Class "K1" 2–6–0s (baby Bongos) were a familiar sight on relief expresses, especially to Clacton." No 62051 stands in sunlight and shade awaiting departure. May 24th 1958. (*Photo* – F. Hornby)

Below: Class "B17/1" No 61634 "HINCHINGBROOKE" attracts schoolboy attention, waiting to leave on April 24th 1956. (*Photo* – N. L. Browne)

Above: A reasonably clean class "K3" No 61953 stands in the company of two class "307" (originally 1,500 volts) E.M.U.s October 1958. (*Photo* – A. J. Pike)

Below: The "essence" of Liverpool Street is captured in this view of the "Day Continental" preparing to leave hauled by class "B17/1" No 61631 "SERLBY HALL" on June 1st 1956. (*Photo* – R. K. McKenny)

Class "J69/1" No 68633 receives attention in the company of a "Brush" type 2 diesel (class "31") awaiting departure on a down train, during May 1960. Even though diesels were making their presence felt by this time, the old Great Eastern flavour was still in evidence.
(*Photo* – J. A. C. Kirke)

Above: "Standard" class "6" No 72009 "CLAN STEWART" poses at Liverpool Street on September 20th 1958. The loco was on loan from Carlisle Kingmoor for trials over the Great Eastern section. Being basically unsuccessful it was soon returned.
(*Photo* – F. Hornby)

Below: In complete contrast to No. 68619, "J69/1" No 68613 on station pilot duties. September 20th 1958. (*Photo* – F. Hornby)

Above: A wet day at Liverpool Street, steam, and smoke mingle with the odour of fish as class "B17/6" No 61646 "GILWELL PARK" heads a down express to Clacton. June 7th 1954. On the left is "Standard" 4MT No 76031. (*Photo* – F. Hornby)

Below: The late 1950s heralded the arrival of diesels to Liverpool Street. "Brush" type 2 No D5515 is on a down express. In the background an unidentified class "B1 is also ready to leave. Empty stock in the foreground is about to be removed by class "N7/3" No 69726. October 1958. (*Photo* – A. J. Pike)

Above: An R.C.T.S. "Invicta" special is preparing to leave Liverpool Street on September 12th 1956. Class "J69s" Nos 68630/68639 are hauling the train via the East London line to Blackheath. (*Photo* – F. Hornby)

Below: Sunlight and shadows, typical Liverpool Street atmosphere. "Britannia Pacific" No 70006 "ROBERT BURNS" and class "N7/3" No 69677 photographed during August 1951. (*Photo* – A. J. Pike)

Class "N7/3" No 69725 was one of eight surviving "N7s"at the end of steam in September 1962. In this view taken on June 17th 1958, the loco is preparing to leave on a surburban train comprised of Gresley articulated coaches. (*Photo* – P. Hay)

Above: A view of the Liverpool Street turntable during August 1951. Class "B1" No 61300 is being turned. (*Photo* – A. J. Pike)

Below: An unusual angle on class "B17/6" No 61664 "LIVERPOOL". Note the cleanliness of the locomotive and the inevitable "spotters". (*Photo* – J. A. C. Kirke)

Class "B17/1" No 61647 "HELMINGHAM HALL" makes an impressive picture on the Liverpool Street turntable on a sunny day during May 1958.
(*Photo* – J. A. C. Kirke)

Above: Class "B1" No 61226 photographed at Liverpool Street on a sunny October 15th 1960. (*Photo* – F. Hornby)

Below: Class "B17/4" No 61653 "HUDDERSFIELD TOWN" of Cambridge (fitted with a K3 type chimney) stands at Liverpool Street in the Spring sunshine with class "K2" No 61721 (with early B.R., lettering still on the tender). May 11th 1951. (*Photo* – P. J. Kelley)

Above: June 1959. Class "B1" No 61270 is photographed between trains at Liverpool Street. (*Photo* – A. J. Pike)

Below: "Britannia Pacifics" awaiting turns of duty at Liverpool Street on May 1960 No 70010 "OWEN GLENDOWER" is in the foreground. (*Photo* – F. Hornby)

Above: Another brace of "J69s". No 68630 (pilot) and No 68612 leave Liverpool Street for the East London line with a Loughton-Brighton excursion on July 4th 1954. (*Photo* – P. J. Kelley)

Below: When Stratford shed cleaned an engine, the job was always carried out to perfection, no exception to the rule is Class "B12/3" No 61576 waiting complete with the Railway Enthusiasts Club "Suffolk Venturer" headboard, prior to a special run on September 30th 1956. (*Photo* – F. Hornby)

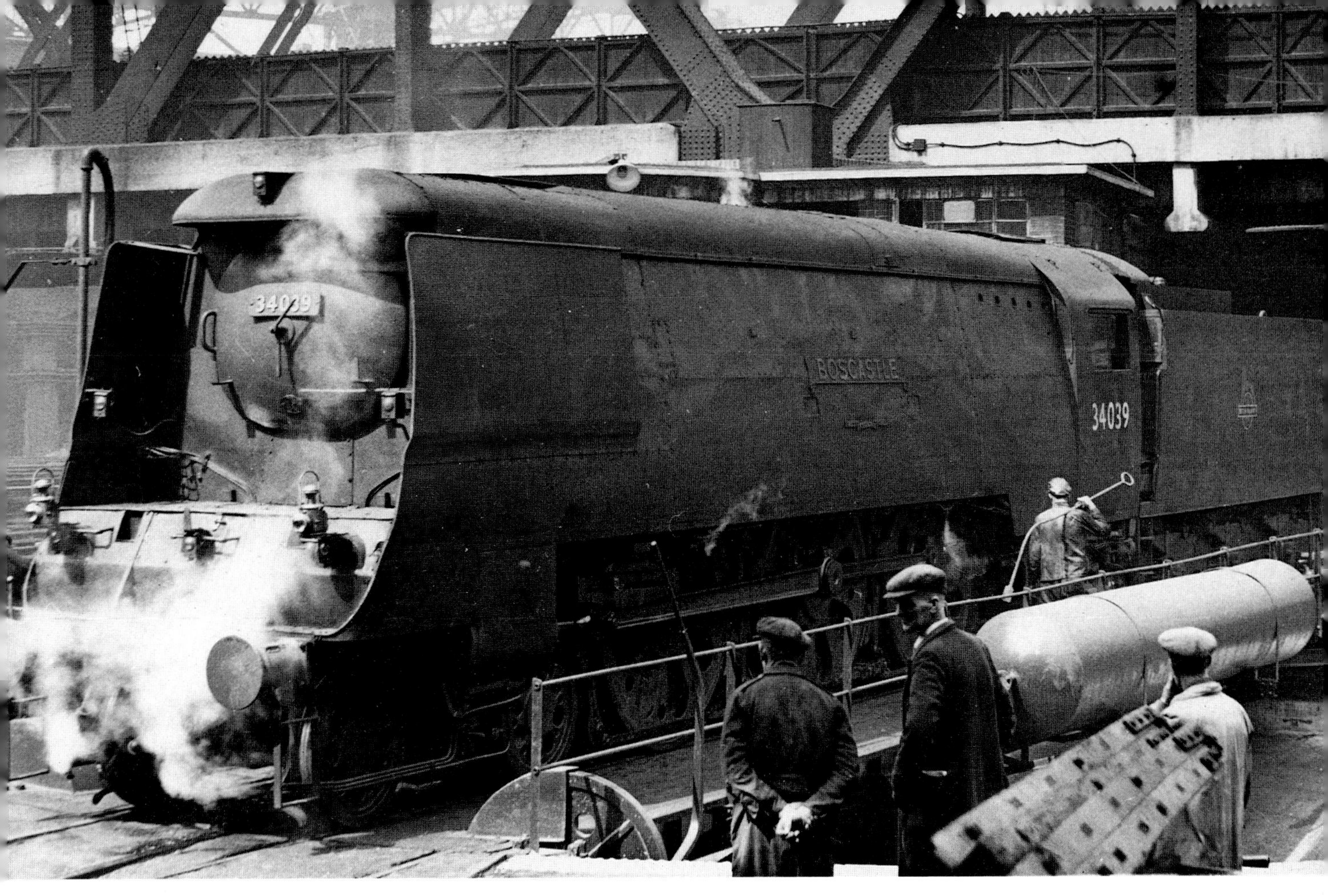

Above: "West Country" class No 34039 is the centre of attraction on the turntable at Liverpool Street. May 11th 1951. The engine was on loan from the Southern Region to access "Pacific" performance on G.E. metals, prior to the introduction of "Britannias".
(*Photo* – P. J. Kelley)

Below: Another view of 34039 "BOSCASTLE" on the engine dock, Liverpool Street. May 11th 1951. (*Photo* – P. J. Kelley)

Above: Bishopsgate Goods Station. September 6th 1953. Immaculate class "D16/3" No 62567 is being prepared for an R.C.T.S. "East Anglian" special. (*Photo* – F. Hornby)

Below: The R.C.T.S. "East Anglian" special (ex-Bishopsgate Goods) is recorded entering Bethnal Green behind class "D16/3" No 62567 on September 6th 1953. (*Photo* – P. J. Kelley)

Above: Another memorable R.C.T.S. special (undertaken in appalling weather) featured former LT&S. 4-4-2T No 80 (B.R. No 41966), celebrating the centenary of the London, Tilbury and Southend Railway. The train is seen passing Bethnal Green on a dismal March 11th 1956. (*Photo* – P. J. Kelley)

Below: An unidentified class "J69" passes a "modernisation" hoarding near Stratford with vans, February 27th 1959. (*Photo* – F. Hornby)

Above: Class "J68" No 68652 trundles a short freight towards Bishopsgate past Bethnal Green. September 20th 1958.
(*Photo* – F. Hornby)

Below: "Britannia Pacifics" did some of their best work on the Great Eastern, where they were held in high esteem by footplate crews. No 70034 "THOMAS HARDY" thunders up Bethnal Green bank on the down "Hook Continental" (8.00pm ex-Liverpool Street). June 29th 1955.
(*Photo* – P. J. Kelley)

Above: A diverted Liverpool Street–Enfield Town train headed by class "N7/5" No 69665 passes Stratford. June 7th 1959.
(*Photo* – N. L. Browne)

Below: Class "L1" No 67702 on a diverted train to Hertford East passes Stratford. June 7th 1959. (*Photo* – F. Hornby)

Above: The 5.19pm Liverpool Street–Cambridge train passes Angel Road, June 29th 1955. The loco is class "K3" No 61801.
(*Photo* – P. J. Kelley)

Below: Angel Road again. Class "N7/5" No 69652 is on the down 5.23pm Liverpool Street–Hertford East train. June 29th 1955.
(*Photo* – P. J. Kelley)

Above: The fireman is obviously busy in this view of class "B17/6" No 61613 "WOODBASTWICK HALL" passing Stratford with a down express. June 7th 1959. (*Photo* – F. Hornby)

Below: An up express passes Stratford with class "K3" No 61959 in charge. Note the G.C.R. carriage next to the loco. August 11th 1956. (*Photo* – F. Hornby)

Above: Stratford, August 20th 1955. An up express rattles through hauled by Class "B17/1" No 61634 "HINCHINGBROOKE".
(*Photo* – F. Hornby)

Below: Stratford Motive Power Depot was the shed which served Liverpool Street. During the 1920s nearly 500 engines were allocated there. In this view class "B1" No 61399 is cleaned in readiness to work the Royal train. April 30th 1956.
(*Photo* – P. J. Kelley)

A sight to behold – class "E4" No 62797 and class "J17" No 65561 both just out of works, pictured at Stratford, January 17th 1954. (*Photo* – P. J. Kelley)

Ex-G.E.R. class "J66s" as Departmental Nos 31 and 32 (originally L.N.E.R. Nos 7313/7281 respectively, B.R. Nos 68382/68370 at Stratford, October 26th

Class "N7/5" No 69668 approaches Stratford Low level on April 15th 1961. Note the magnificent elevated signal box and the junction with Stratford East Curve.
(*Photo* – A. E. Bennett)

During October 1959, East side pilot No 68619 was repainted in G.E.R. blue livery retaining its B.R. emblem, with a G.E.R. coat of arms below the

On a very damp November 11th 1960, East side pilot No 68619 is photographed preparing for an R.C.T.S. railtour. (*Photo* – J. A. C. Kirke)

Railtours around the London area from Liverpool Street became very popular during the late fifties. "J69/1" No 68577 is at New Cross Gate with the

Above: The East London Railtour, organised by the R.C.T.S. April 14th 1951, has just arrived at North Woolwich, with no less than eight corridor coaches hauled by class "J69/1" No E8619 (this engine was in L.N.E.R. green livery from 1948 to 1953).
(*Photo* – P. J. Kelley)

Below: One of the famous boat-train headboards, the "Hook Continental", fitted to "Britannia" No 70037 "HEREWARD THE WAKE". May 24th 1958.
(*Photo* – N. L. Browne)

Liverpool Street was rather unique, it enjoyed a love hate relationship with the travelling public and never set out to be anything it wasn't. On misty days the atmosphere was almost intolerable as processions of "N7" tanks waited with Westinghouse pumps panting to charge up Bethnal Green bank. This photograph was taken in April 1957, and again really does not need describing.

(*Photo* – A. J. Willmott)